− R.

SMYTHE LIBR

Carcanet titles by the same author

The Island Normal
The Children of Separation

Freeborn John

BRIAN JONES

"Ah, I see," said the Inspector. "You have
misunderstood me. You are under arrest, certainly, but
that need not hinder you going about your business."
Kafka, *The Trial*

CARCANET

First published in 1990 by
Carcanet Press Limited
208-212 Corn Exchange Buildings
Manchester M4 3BQ

British Library Cataloguing in Publication Data
Jones, Brian *1938-*
  Freeborn John
  I. Title
  821'.914

ISBN 0-85635-895-9

The publisher acknowledges financial assistance from
the Arts Council of Great Britain.

Typeset in 10pt Palatino by Bryan Williamson, Darwen, Lancashire
Printed in England by SRP Ltd., Exeter

821.914
R62886X

For Bill and Ada, my parents
and for
the Kinship of Jones

...to learn to what extent the effort to think one's
own history can free thought from what it silently
thinks, and so enable us to think differently.

Foucault, *The Use of Pleasure*

Contents

Introductory
1638: Freeborn John

'If people knew the times where they were cast,
they'd look about them:
see the great Squares grown shambles, note
how Execution, flagrantly empowered,

lops ears that hear, melts eyes that see.
The main ignore
the iron in the flesh and soul, twitch down
the brim of tact, and squint the ground.

Close in chambers, men take the oaths
by which they are accused. England
staggers, debauched by Law. Injustice
prowls among the orchard-trees,

serves up the ale, and clinks the wage.
I see honour only among graves,
the stone fleets of the just dead,
the traffic of deceitless bone;

and in him, the one they flogged
from Fleet to pillory, his hands
still showering to the heedless bands
sweet seditious leaves, new-pressed,

till clamped beside his head. His mouth
then cried 'Wake, England!' – till with wadding tamped.
At which – O wonderful – I saw his feet
risk their small liberty to stamp . . . stamp . . . stamp.'

Stansted Sonnets

for my father

1.

At the War Memorial

autumn 1987

Together like yoked oxen we lean
into this tailgate slam of tempest.
An equal brevity of staunched stride.
A muscular understanding after
lame decades. We have entered the kinship
of Jones: one of the snapped tap-roots
of anonymous names – Betts, Blackman, Bowyer,
– curt mossed laterals, from which flowers
this svelte youth, whose beauty was the profile
insouciantly sought in mirrors
by the generation whose gas its flame
was lit to sweeten. Between spread, raised arms
crackles a leap of frond: Peace,
on which, in our line of sight, he hangs nailed.

2.
The Bronze Figure

His half-stride is that archaic
hesitation towards consciousness.
He broaches the trance of myth and enters
history's squalor, where perennial bronze
bleeds emerald down marble towards
the rising moss, skirting white islands
at the heart of names, pure o's, small complete
moons lapped by a stained sky, an essence
persisting, a bequest of nothing, innocence,
something gone, a moan gusted across meadows,
endless, broken. Flint in wind-skimmed furrows.
Eyes of bone. At the frond's ragged tips
drips black debris, like gouts from legendary
chopped boughs. Insistent sacrifice.

3.
After Hurricane

A stumped timber statuary bleeds
memory down the bleached lanes: Constable's
moist collusive vision, murdered
by the swingeing tail of tempest. Helmeted,
a madam clops her Arab-faced blond mare
fastidiously in a shimmying finesse
of broken boughs. An embalmed
dislocation staggering for poise.
The churchyard wall is breached
to a cold flick of flint. I imagine
outriders of the New Order pausing
to gaze down into the heartlands
of the self-defeated. England's face
truly surfacing. A brutal, frightened stare.

4.
My Father's Faith

Remember Bevan? a haughty blub
of tilted head bobbing on its sibilants
at the cavernous end of a barn. An owl
at bay. The fine contempt of the doomed.
I stood shoulder-to-knee with you
at that by-election. Truth had a start
of eighteen over the ravening pack –
Fear, Loss of Nerve, Self-Interest. Surely
God could swing it! Every night I prayed
to His commonsense – Who could only plump
for the future, and gave His nod
to a watchful dwarf in glasses. You wept,
hearing clipped Attlee's curt goodbye.
God after God packing into the past.

5.
Get-together

When Joneses meet, they embrace in a great
sigh of alignment. They drag a honky-tonk
into a pool of tears and vamp The Gipsy
and Shine on Harvest Moon. Men kiss men
most unEnglishly. Nervous new-Jones spouses
are initiated with reminiscence and huge
scarlet and mauve hearts on the cheek. The dead –
squandered by war, tuberculosis, suicide;
and the six-week-old great aunt, who never
took shape, except in memories – return
in whispered, tearful corners. A powerhouse
throbs in the night – all those clear
unsullied eyes, those springs sudden as truth
welling from bodies bought but not wholly given.

6.
Family Album

A tea-gold face, a several-times great
grandfather, sharp enough to prize
a new contraption that sucks the soul
and sends it purely fading from inessentials
into the future: pale, furious, visionary
eyes, persisting in my eighteen-year-old
virgin grandmother, her winged shoulders and tilted
chin cleaving onward, and in her nut-shrunk
monkey-face, bitter among three children
six years later. An heirloom of unsatisfied
uncompromised requirement, an unblinking
arrogant insistence, of which a distant
uncle was robbed in Flanders, an aunt
died uncured in a house of the mad.

7.
A View from Stansted

A cold vision is settling into place: barbed
certainties that mark red in the balance-sheet
the questioner, the immigrant, the reflective;
it crushes discourse beneath its monologue
and proves dreams pathology; sees us scrabbling
on a dying planet and sneers Why not? Colonised
England wakes to find itself facing itself
in the rigid lines of winners and losers.
Its vaunting irony, its booted curled-lip
humour, its scything realism that takes
every thought at the knee, its trip-wire horror
of all touch except tickle and rape, are coming
home to us down the inevitable lanes
to claim their birthright and to wear our face.

8.

Betts, Blackman, Bowyer, Brown, Briggs,
Green, Jones, Walker: we have been
available as headstones, prompt as fodder;
defused by an Africa Star, a gilt watch,
tits on the breakfast table, and a need
for a V Reg Vauxhall. None but our lovers
wept at our scattered limbs. We kicked
Indians in the stomach, Gatlinged
Zulus, jeered black subtle wingers. We reached
for the juices on dangled hooks, and fuelled
the juggernaut with our blood and choice.
England is posthumous with our fidelity.
We stand among broken trees as Outriders
rev their machines to cruise towards our Yes.

9.

They are coming, father. They have settled
helmets over their brains and kicked
machines to life. They warble across
the tarmac lanes. I want you to start
speaking now. I want you to tell
your story endlessly like a faultless
loop. I want the album open
at the sepia but glaring eyes
of all our generations. As they arrive
to force our door like confident guests,
be there, in that magisterial chair,
a history spread on your lap,
with me, my children, and the framed ghosts
attentive, like drinkers at a source.

Caesar's Progress

This is your enemies' country which they took
in the small hours an age before you woke
Geoffrey Hill: *The Mystery of the Charity of Charles Peguy*

The Images of Caesar

So many bald-eyed impostors
gazing down the echoing galleries of the world

all with their advocates:
Stoffels favouring that brutal-jowled

bust in Naples; Nieburger
that green basalt block in Berlin,

narrow-skulled and blunt of vision
(like Nieburger).

Others quite failing to see
how a clamped hysteria

or a louche and fleshy menace
points to Cicero, or Sejanus.

I can only wearily reiterate
'This is the one':

He outstares the changing light
and makes no plea

to be understood, liked, or forgiven.
He has shed blood without remorse

for the sake of some greater good.
His smile plays like a cold sunlight

on the pit of human failings.
I return day after day

and watch for hours
as he yearns savagely through the thickets of time.

Pre-History of the Tribe

From the scrupulous care with which they buried
Their dead – the alignment of bodies, set like
Tubers in furrows, the clutch of tools at hand,
And the female figures, featureless except
For their great pods of belly – we may infer
That they fancied that the soul would still endure.
Or something like the soul something like endure.
And this despite the frailty of their handiwork
In a context of beasts: lions, bears, gluttons,
Wolves and their fellows; and the demoniacal
Lava and flame belching from what is now to us
Rock and extinct. At this distance they appear
The least harmful fruit of earth, nervous to assume
The claws and godhead of their inheritance.

Caesar Punishes the Tribe

'Unhand them, to grope their way as best they can
Through the forests. But, first of all, unhand them.'
I cannot imagine the sound of blade through bone
Again and again, countlessly repeating
Its shock through the echoing groves. Ripe and unripe
Stalks reaped by the stub blades, until the glade floors
Thicken to lakes with the crisped fingers of the drowned
Who moan stumped and dripping. But I can conceive
Their tenderness to one another who cannot
Touch, who have only pain and intent and words.
'The aspect of this region was, of course, so
Very different from that beautiful France
With which we are so familiar: the gay land
Of picturesque old towns, aweful cathedrals,
Of cornfields, and vineyards, and sunny hamlets.'

Caesar's Progress

No conqueror concerns himself with questions
Of ethnology: the word is no more in
His vocabulary than in a poet's.
Both forge relationships, not acknowledge them.
But we may speculate on what manner of men
Peered through shaggy eyebrows from the rocky heights
As slowly, insensibly, civilisation
Moved on, with clank of iron, creak of leather.
Enthusiastic, impulsive, quick-witted,
Childishly inquisitive and credulous,
Joyous in victory, despondent in defeat,
Impatient of law and discipline, they were
Ill-equipped to resist that high-principled
Juggernaut crushing roads of scruple and bone.

The Schooling of the Tribe

They stooped to the yoke, and then arose
With the degraded cunning of the unhanded.
Phlegm laced the lord's sauces.
Piss frothed the ale. They gauged

Their skills to the just-unpunishable.
The guts of their speech rotted with irony.
Manhood proved itself with fists. Women
Starred in ritual humiliations.

Yearly the tribe trekked south
As permitted, along permitted
Roads, for schooling in those dream landscapes
Promised to the full sleep of servitude:

Through sunflower-fields where adoring faces
Lifted as one towards the brazen
Hanging Christs, and poppies and marguerites
Spattered like transfigured blood and tears

The iron roots of the cross. Water-cannon
Like generous, opened arteries
Pumped long glittering ostrich-plumes
To seed the air and haze the lolling

Tongues of maize. In island cemeteries,
Embedded softly in fields like natural groves,
Porcelain petals winked, and chrysanthemums
Smouldered remembered love upon the graves.

Here were a people grappled to verities –
Fruit and gathering and proper dying –
Stooped over fields and graves beneath the sky's yoke,
Free of that savage purity of self-regard

With which the tribe slunk by, poisoned
By memory: the hoarded violence
In children's eyes as they fingered
Bayonets raked from the beet-fields;

The sea-stopped edge of their world
Where curt headstones, lozenge after lozenge,
Stepped off infinitely in bureaucratic
De-creation. Sun, and bulging peppery

Wine would be theirs for a month,
And the lectures of salt-rimed sensuality,
And the amnesia of the raped palate,
From which every autumn they returned

A little more inclined like sunflower-heads
To the sun of the inevitable, to a brutal
Approval of law and order, and to direct
Visitors to the historic war-graves.

Caesar Chooses Leaders from the Tribe

The grudge of tribute. The sloping
Shoulders brooding on rage. The whining
Down-wind voices of the hunched women.
These badged the tribe, became the inheritance

Of the watchful young squatting at the hearth
Raising their eyes from Latin or the plains of History.
Most slammed the books like doors, and mimicked
Slouch at street-corners, and sour-handed work,

Setting up homes where they engaged each other
In speechless violence until both died.
A few made sense of what they read, gathering
Tongues and perspectives. These were rewarded

And watched. Very carefully watched. They rose
Like corks inevitably, until the time
Set for their trial, known as interview.
Here, they were given words to use: Control,

Leadership, Decision-making, Management.
And words to interpret: Negotiation,
Consultation, Team. All were punished.
Some with preferment and the memory

Of wholeness. Some with wholeness and a desk
In a cobwebbed corner of a province. Some
With flogging till they were insensible
And then beheading. Those sent to provinces

Were watched. Very carefully. It was suspected
That they might correspond, or meet each year
Murmuring to one another on a beach under the sun.
They received regularly details of new posts

And dates of interview.

Caesar Feeds

He explodes grapes against muscular
Cheeks, and stares in gloom at predictable
Culminations of lust. He is stone-bored.
The dancers flickering through vinous webs,
The floating gauzes, the unctuous wine-
Laved glottals of flattery. He craves
More and different. Item: a minor clerk
Scrolling fraudulent entries for love of
Caesar in a room beyond surveillance.
Item: a poet redeemed by exile,
His rhymes purged of the warp of bitterness.
Item: a peasant sweeping, to songs of Caesar,
A glittering curve of seed across his earth.
He sighs. Praetorian guards finger their swords.

Action Plan from Caesar's Inspectorate

He offers his hands
We chop him at the wrist

He phrases a meaning
We invert it in commas

He sees the situation
We call it paranoia

He falls in love
We maintain it is illegal

He embarks on a search
We publicise his uncertainty

He observes boundaries
We declare him obstructive

He embraces wholeness
We put him on an island

He moves inward
We announce him mad

Drinking Song of Caesar's Inspectors

A man
settles his hat
and walks
to a car.

Nothing
has happened
except
except

the changed
perspectives
in the room
he left,

a face
bereft
of vision,
the walls

spattered
with words
absurd
and apt,

two hands
slack
with purpose
gone,

the brains
emptied,
and what
remains

free
to slam
a door
and drive

through the rest
of life
as if
alive.

Caesar's Laureate

His first task
Was to judge their competition.
They gave him a hundred poems
All trapped in what they should be.

Autumn was there, and God,
Three grandmothers,
And assorted cats that gave
Undying affection.

Three won the prizes,
The others approval,
On a night among smiles
And wine.

The main prize, of course,
Was him standing there,
Preened despite himself
With new shoes and a crease.

He screamed all the way home,
Beating the steering wheel.
He spewed down the pan
But nothing would go away.

And there was no poem among that hundred
that understood him.
And there was no memory of a face
Among that crowd that disbelieved him.

Application for a Post in Caesar's Bureaucracy

Sir (or Madam), I have the politic
skill that dismantles the true
answers to questions lobbed at me
and returns what you currently
approve. Also, over the years,
I have quite successfully
cut myself in two

which empowers me
to face both ways, smile
in all directions, and not know
if I am coming or going.
No-one believes anything about me
except my power, which is,
of course, yours, sir (or madam).

My 'no' can sound
like 'We'll see' to the strong
and 'Tomorrow' to the insistent.
My cringe is perfectly clear
to all offices on the upper
floor, and their anger
panics me to punish

the weak (for whom I am developing
a ferret-sharp appetite).
My two suits are appropriately
stained at the crotch
and anally, and blotched
on the collar with a steady
fall of hair and scurf.

I learn rolling on my back
from my two dogs,
deception from my children.
My wife's craven inadequacy
teaches me so much
about the needs
and history of women.

I am, of course, not a complete
shit, nor a total yes-man
yet. Somewhere I have anguish
but not too much
and it is not all that important,
sir (or madam). Those I sell
down the river

I do grieve for:
it is always so unnecessary.
It needs only a little bending
this way and that way
and everything can be
as it should be, whatever
that may be.

I intend to put together
a volleyball team
to represent the service.
It is not my fault
if those who cannot
grub or spike are those
we can well do without:

that simply indicates
a deep pattern in things.
I am quite prepared
to offer my counselling
to the inadequate, all we require
is a willingness to learn
what's what, whatever that what is

or what you might
change it to.
I believe in good practice,
but there are many ways
to skin a cat, and who's
to tell who's right
except those whose right

it is to tell us?
I like people who smile
(but not knowing smiles),
buoyant, optimistic people, preferably
women with long crossed legs
who smile most of the time, but know
how to weep when it gets rough.

I can, therefore, affirm
my sadism, my skills
of sycophancy and coat-turning.
My record proves my paranoia,
and my referees are eloquent
testimony to my hollowness
in which orders are echoed with pure

unadulterating accuracy.
I am prepared to move
anywhere at any time
for any purpose.
I feel I am ready now
to shoulder greater burdens
of servitude

and crave the opportunity
of interview.
I once worked for you
but trust you will find me
sufficiently faceless
as to be utterly unrememberable,
sir, (or madam).

Poets chainsmoke, but live to eighty
if they can evade the amorous
clasp of the gods:

'It's all a matter of the object
of your regard.
If your attention

is wholly drawn to your waistline,
the possibility of exploding moles,
and what is written

on the side of fag-packets,
you have no chance'.
Poets watch

white sheets of paper
for the first signs of words
like rare birdprints

breaking the silence of a snowfield:
'We are observers. Observers are wafer-thin,
translucent and organless.

There is little room
for death to breed'.
Poets do not run around the block

in pursuit of sweat.
Fear provides.
They do not patrol

highstreets for style.
Never climb ladders
to unblock a gutter.

Poets would not be seen
dead at a funeral:
'Time passing

is in every tap
of the typewriter,
every scrapped biro'.

Poets enjoy fruit
with worms in, hence
they escape the chemical

perfection of supermarkets.
Despair wakes them early, so death
never catches them napping.

Their lovers say
they have no heart,
so where can be the attack?

Since no-one reads a poet,
there is no litigation,
no imprisonment, no hanging.

Since a poet
barely exists
he can barely die.

The status quo
is what we propose:
they might live long

but pose no threat.
When they think they are political,
they are symbolic,

metaphorical, atavistic,
and are read primarily
for their vowel-sounds.

They think very highly of themselves
and their chances of immortality
(see our quotations)

but since this is of little social significance
and very few had any
inkling of invasion

let alone conquest,
our review is brief,
far shorter

than the one we are presently
engaged on:
'Political Recalcitrance among Librarians'.

Caesar's Circular, after Implementation of the Four Year Plan

Nothing radical has happened.
And in any case it is now all over.
People have a thousand reasons
To be happier and more productive than before.
It is hoped that words like 'buoyant'
And 'optimistic'
Will be found more frequently
In all reports.
People can still meet,
Of course they can.
It is just that records will need to be kept
To facilitate payment of expenses.
As for the malicious rumour
About centralised control –
Well, we are investigating that.
Of course we have confidence in our procedures:
The key appointments were made
By a thrifty greengrocer from the West Province
And a practical mother-of-four
From the East – the sort of people
Who know what's what, and who were voted in
By fifty-one percent of the seventeen percent
Who voted. Those who have disappeared
Received, we can assure you,
Appropriate recompense. The demoted
Will receive counselling in our Retraining Centres
And in time will apply for posts
Like different men and women.
If anyone has any queries or concerns,
Please let me know in writing
Taking care to indicate name, address,
Post code and telephone number,
So that I have no difficulty
In responding at once.

For a Nativity

1.

Every birth is the premonitory pang
in Caesar's heart, his fatal flaw.
He curses the legions into double-pace.
His spotlights sweep the barbed compounds.

2.

The animals understand:
something has happened small and shouting
on straw unexpectedly that needs
to be muzzled upright onto its own legs.

3.

A winter event:
frost-seeded furrows,
ice-veins clamping the world's heat,
bloodberries spattering the snow insistently.

4.

There is the pattering of tiny feet:
it is the Imperial Extinguisher
scuttling to every stable in the land
with the official Aims and Objectives.

5.

Birth distils what remains of hope:
the water-drop at which the dam cracks,
the outrider of depths,
the dream that haunts noontide.

La Trahison d'un Clerc

Compulsion and enforcement may make a confused mass
of dissembling hypocrites, not a congregation of believers.
William Walwyn: *A Whisper in the Ear of Mr Thomas Edwards*

1.

You must know, from the outset, I am resolutely
unclubbable. Please do not be-comrade or be-friend
me. I am prompted by Puckishness. I wish to prove
that when Secrecy racks its great presses down
an irresistible sweetness extrudes, drawing
all manner of insects, you being one.

2.

The Chief Executive is wetting himself. He ranges
our dismal corridors howling 'Leaks!' like a deprived
Welshman on Saint David's day, or an indigent plumber.
It is a source of deepest glee for me to disturb
his dreams (where, I am sure, he merely programmes himself
like a good computer, to conduct the reign of terror –
I really cannot imagine him enjoying
a towards-dawn tumescence, although perhaps 'cost-efficient'
throbs and grows quite luminous in the small hours.)
Attached, a memo to the disciplinary think-tank.

3.

Find enclosed a confidential proposal
to sell your buildings, and to loose you down the wind
for market-forces to prey on. I am deeply offended
by the constant mis-use of 'will' for 'shall'
and by the structural absence of the possessive apostrophe.
The latter bespeaks no respect for proper
ownership, and a preference (also exemplified
in the refusal to use full stops with abbreviations)
for unseemly haste, curtailment of courtesies,
and disregard for procedures. Use this document
as you will to wreak the utmost damage.

4.

The Chief Executive sees himself (did he but know it)
as a Vergil of Market Forces, rewriting all our stories
into an epic clarity and persuasiveness; leading the tribe
from a bankrupt homeland (justly in ashes) towards
a cost-efficient new foundation, ringing with Roman virtue.
What I find distasteful is the absence of Vergilian
silvered sadness, the decent trace of tears.

5.

In this paper (which names all those employees
suspected of resisting the new culture, and who
are to be purged in the next review) you will find
a flagrant misuse of terms. Students are called
'customers', and seats of learning 'properties'.
Pursuing this logic, Caveat Emptor should be engraved
on the portal of my old College! Really, my dear,
this might be witty, emanating from a more rounded
gentry, but from the arrivistes who manage
this mutilated province, it amounts to boorish
bullying. Please use your incendiary skills
to fire the thews of hoi polloi and oik.

6.

You will have observed that, on the very day
the KGB produced a promotional video,
PIS (our Public Information Service) launched
its upbeat, demotic tabloid, full of buoyant
zombies. I am outraged. Although the higher echelons
were diplomatically not featured, nevertheless,
in some deep if distasteful way, I am a colleague
of all those smiling faces, the Province's employees,
whose lives this rag distorts to advertisement.
Like Maisie, from Accounts, pictured at her Amstrad,
smiling, who spent her holiday tramping the coast
to raise money for the inmates of one of *our* homes!
Fair Maisie – wait for it – slipped and broke a leg
while fording a flood! Some cretinous passing jogger
hitched her up and piggybacked her (ouch!)
to the nearest village. Now, back at her desk, she plans
to abseil down the face of Provincial Hall!
Really! I mean! . . . If you can use your subversive skills
to disseminate this directive, photocopied
from a jotter, which outlines in barbaric grammar
procedures for privatising care of the gormless,
you will make an old man happy – and I might even
offer my grinning fizzog for rag number two.

7.

I pissed next to the Chief Executive today.
I am gratified that my grin quite staunched his jet.
He struggled to expel, wagged, and gave up.
A minor triumph for the natural aristocrats!
He growled something about the weather, as though
meteorology were the one thing he could not control.
I quoted Propertius to myself and answered nothing,
then appropriated the one washbasin graced with soap.
This must all sound petty, but one must grasp
the smallest victories in the face of the cosmic
humiliations to which one is daily subject. Talking of which,

here are details of the closure of your department
and guidance as to how to avoid standard recompense
in the face of union demands. If you should go,
please inform me a.s.p. of your successor.
I am so tickled by these wicked games!

8.

So. No quarter given. You stood and were counted
out; while I maintain the irony of an oblique
unfocussed stance, like this dust-thronged angle of sun
bewildering the space I intend to inhabit
until I step into a pension. I know, now, that
is terrible: I watched the student spread his arms
and jig before the tank like a carnival cross;
and, as my friend lay dying (I've told no-one this)
loudspeaker vans traversed the city, exhorting us
to embrace change, as though we were not universes,
as though he were not a universe who filled his space
with elegance and tact; as though we were just function
not mystery; as though we could eradicate
our stories like a tape-machine. My whole schooling
was to survive. You can expect no more of me.
I shall remember you as someone I might have shared
some drinks with, but I suspect we have different
tastes and, although comrades in battle,
we might have found an evening a touch de trop.
Since I like my flat the way it is, and regular
Medoc, and visits to the sun, I hope my missives
remain unintercepted, and that your replacement
is trustworthy. Be all that as it may, I intend
to leak as frequently as someone prostate-plagued.
Please remember that, at your desk in the far province.

Exiled Voices

The greatest violence done to people in our
society is to rob them of a public life.
David Smail: *Taking Care*

1.

Scarred and thinned down this crackling line
you are finally a voice they could not make disappear.
It is as if I had stumbled on Villon's cell

the night before the promised gibbet:
a mouth close to earth, insistent on words.
But I see a hesitant host on New Year's Eve

bearing a fragrant curry and cool mint
and hoping to give pleasure.
I feel a rare loss with this click of your absence.

I feel a hopelessness for my species.
When that New Year struck
our clinking glasses made a true connection.

2.

It is Spring in this province.
I fill my attention with crocuses:
nests of gaping fledglings,
single-minded throats of zealots,

vaginal welcomings.
This garden hosts my last metaphors,
that act of colonising emptiness
for which I am losing taste.

I have a mistress with tresses
like a tree-shadowed waterfall
etcetera.
She is irrelevant in daylight

where I budget, under supervision,
the approved educational needs
of approved learners.
My body is provided for –

my teeth, my guts, my vision.
I am learning to use
the approved waste-bins
for my dreams: the melon-slice beaches,

the hot rocks above the sea,
the reeking night-clubs,
and the concerts with oriental soloists.
My transport is a twin-carburettor

overhead camshaft four-wheel drive
automatic coupé. I have
a casual user allowance
which I am learning to fiddle.

I have fantasised you
into someone who will understand.
The only reader
of the only thing I write.

Are you there?
I have received only silence from you
for so long. The reports
from your province

are approved and depressing.
I need your voice. I will understand
any code. If you do not write,
I will decipher that.

Two glistening blackbirds
are scuffling for space. They make
this lawn an emblematic
field of defiant

memory. Some ideas must be
ubiquitous as birds,
bright and pert as in
the distant regions of their coining.

3.

Every night, I am visited
by a ghost of buried tenderness:

in gusts and spasms
she delectably settles words on my tongue

in the deep lost hours of sleep,
vanishing as I rise to speak.

When I walk my fury like a dog
through Caesar's woodland

she catches my breath with the beginnings
of melting tunes that have no development.

Suddenly, in my magisterial green
chair, where I rigidly brood

on our ambushed naive intent,
she insinuates into my muscles

a brimming forgiveness
soon spilt.

We chose the wrong weapons so carefully
from the Imperial Catalogue.

If I have a final journey
it will be mining inward

to lead her lovingly
into unreserved light

to be a spasm in Caesar's heart,
his fatal flaw.

4.

'The political context of our defeat':
I struggle to keep your words close to my heart

but they are like birds in autumn,
aimed elsewhere and swiftly vanishing.

They leave me in my familiar landscape:
a small boy in a drizzling fallout of guilt,

his hand in his pants or up a girl's
awaiting the chop.

We attempted the hero's world of arena and boardroom
but I never expected otherwise or more

than the happenings of this room:
a windswept desk and an empty phone.

It is a rehearsal for death
for which I have always been prepared

who barely managed to live, give or care.
And did I make Caesar tremble?

A few offered freedoms, a few hours
letting people talk, airing their battered dreams,

finding words that will not be marked out of ten.
We will not be allowed to use those words again.

I expected the juggernaut across my wrists.
I see you as Sisyphus, the world your stone,

shouldering upwards in history's spotlight.
But for me it was always darkness. I was always alone.

5.

They treat us like fools,
setting quite impossible tasks
and insouciantly turning away
to their rooms where the Silver Book
gleams like a blade.

What do they care about our dreams?
Little gracenotes and curlicues
around an iron tune.
They pay us, and life's
as simple as that.

Our room for manoeuvre
is twisting inside our own
contradictions.
Our energy flogs itself
with whips of strategy.

We are too clever by half.
Clauses, parentheses, footnotes,
ironic equivocations.
They went straight through the gates
to the heart of fear,

to the City-centre of self-love,
smiling from their tanks.
Look at our sisters, with their
garlands and blown kisses.
Look. There is your father.

A metal-barrelled pen
is tapping impatiently
upon your annual report.
Who wants to hear such things?
They belong to history and theory,

and warrant only qualifications
to cushion a name.
Spend a sabbatical on these things,
during which time the world
will have moved further

out of reach, into which
you will step blinking
and unaccustomed,
lucky to find your position
still open, narrowing fast.

6.

My passport said 'British'.
I resented that.
The boots slamming on continents.
The cuffs stiff with insensitivity
at the end of jungles.
I wanted to write 'English'
for its sly evasive music
and sensual valleys,
its twists and turns and unlocatable
laconic heart.
But that could not be tolerated.
They had to move me on
like a folk-song into a new setting,
atonal and without atmosphere.
'British' will do for that.

7.

If we had words like 'cell',
'interrogation', and 'been shot',

perhaps we might believe ourselves.
It's hard to live in a fuzzy watercolour

of dragged emphases.
What have we to complain about

except everything which is nothing?
We ought to get on with it

and think ourselves lucky.
If we speak for ourselves

that is poetry with a limited
circulation. If for others,

presumption. Silence has always been
quite good enough. It spawned us

and paid our way among bookshelves.
If we learned other languages

we should go there to speak them.
Life is handed to us on a plate.

It doesn't matter whose head it is.
Our punishment is that it is not ours.

8.

I have chastening news:
One year after slavery was abolished
in the old empire,
lost souls came wailing
to the hacienda

of their former master
begging for servitude.
They presented a book
with six hundred and twenty three reasons.

Perhaps it is time
to cultivate whatever gardens have been allowed us.

9.

Although our topic is pain, remarkably
it is like walking through a favourite garden
pointing out what is special about the flowers
and nodding. Let me tell you that your intent
to hurt by your angry flounce away will not
figure a damn or a jot. To those you would
wound, you have never been otherwise than some
varying indications in red and blue
columns. Your anger, that stain along your hair,
what your hands do at times like this, or how you
painfully yield up certain words – these things
have never counted, and this allows them to take
refuge in moods of quiet satisfaction
in heavily panelled rooms.
                         Our main concern
must be: How do we *stay*? There will be a moment
when they step off the edge of their agenda
and when the woman who is not expected to hear
has cleared their cups and listens. The sun will cook
the panels, and they will have to look somewhere:
at each other differently, or at the doodles
flowering at the edge of their minutes. That is
where I intend to inhabit, blood-boltered.
And are you to be there with me? Shall we try?

Letter from Elsewhere

It was not quite as we'd imagined
when we honed the splendour of consciousness
housed in the bodies of the just:
I approached a sun-thronged lozenge

where woodland opened to a path
that tussocked down to a fordable river.
Water tickled my ankles. A few stones ·
slurred their green rondures. And I emerged

squelching through the pats of cows that were
technically barbarian into the daisies
and buttercups of an alien regime. I had crossed
the Border!

I felt all we'd prefigured
in those smoke-anguished rooms: I sensed
trained on my back the trembling
rifle-sights of death-starved guards.

I knew behind each copse the shaggy
welcoming figures waited with their
torturing altars and backlog of impotence
to be vented on my flesh. But –

the stream chattered gaily away,
cows munched and sputtered,
and if soldiers patrolled a barbed border
and barbarians cared, it was solely

in a collusive myth. So my stomp
through forbidden cowshit was brutally
deflating, warranting no publicity
of departure or arrival. If there are

checks to the foot, they are not located
in trip-wires or snipers, but in a kind
of love, a defining by relationship,
a need to be needed, as a hand

reaching for blackberries expects a thorn
to make an autumn ritual complete.
At last I stood as uneventfully
as hawthorn on the far bank, and the guard

who slammed lead punishingly through me
was Nostalgia: an intense sunlight
on abandoned hills; a song suddenly
perfected on a forgiven tongue. I live

in my chosen dream, have parted company
with the possibility of being elsewhere
but where daylight at this moment gleams.
I have no excuse for desire. And I envy you.

The Cherry Orchard

'I know of no context, religious or political,
in which to set us. Therefore, I describe us as
we are.' – Chekhov

1.

Thoughts from a Home Abroad

'Their vision frugal as their famed landscape:
flint fields, where bouncing tractors scourge
a washed-out blood through the wan stubble;
hedgerows, where sunless berries drag their grit
and birds sputter from rat-tail to rat-tail.
The bomb, Time, has exploded, unqualified
their brute verbs, exposed their moody
intuitions that grazed dream grass, to winter
in a corral of judgment – and still the tribes
muffle themselves on god-stripped holy days
to trudge and gawp, and snuffle under trees,
hunting the truffle, peace; though History sees them
stark on the bald skyline, blatant as witnesses,
broad as a wall, easy to see and hit.'

2.
The Cherry Orchard

Buckled beneath his gut, crunching
superfluous sweetness under Army surplus
boots, he patrols these fairylight late
alleys pleached by dusk. The bequeathed shotgun
waltzes the air, keeping him and England
quiet. Soon he will void both barrels
in cherry-bored mastery, spattering
fruit like brains. A shadow in this lane,
I edge contumacious and licensed
proprietorship; and here, in wishbone pairs,
cherries sway, as though the only route
of freedom for the gift of yielding
ripeness is towards my hands.
A small path. And still forked by choice.

3.
Of a Friend

'Do you dare remember him? He framed
imagination into small courtesies
that people might perform. The wideshouldered
Lords of Practice instituted
public executions and sent his skills
gulping down Mainstreet gutters. Now,
he flies to Sorrento in a fling of overt
disdain, towards the immoral isle of Tiberius
to purge the black scutterings that crawl his eyes:
English fruit. I am left thinking of me,
the face's adjustment before the spotlight falls.
The lanes are still free, between the signs; and cricket
deploys its rapturous codes of silence
on every Green, whitely policing Fact.'

4.
Exits and Entrances

We lean on interruptions: the canted gate
weathered to pure strata of crystal grain,
rooted in bindweed; the honey-glazed pot
poised above the books, jetting prawn-whiskered
barley from a field now under brick –
the whole of contemplation, as dusk
slowly silts the hands for another day.
This preference for pause rather than the route
downhill to consequence, is called
England. It burrows into the Pilgrims'
Way, lured by its muddy tongue to where
sunbursts dance with the motes of granular flies –
slow bubbles hung in a golden cider –
down vistas of decay and quietude.

5.
Budget Day: 1988
for S.

'I had to phone. I'm shaking and feel frightened.
I've been listening to his speech. Suddenly, I became
my neighbour, mobilised with righteousness,
looking in on me – this user of resources,
unworthy of credit, unfit for work,
unretrainable except in awareness.
A furious spotlight moves this way,
dredging for waste. I want you to know
I need you, those coffee-drenched evenings
shored up with old-world distaste
and laced with vision, their celebration
of styleless, longhaired, unexploiting dreams.
Next year – hear me say this – next year he'll grant me
a gun – a bullet for me and an allowance for my child.'

6.

Ignorance

'I've been walking through my nightmare, that unshakeable
seizure of being colonised, of letting it happen.
My laziness bred strangeness everywhere: the lane
towards the orchard rang with the songs of birds
whose names I never learned; trees loomed
through the miasma of my unfocussed love, named
only for the market – apple and cherry;
shrubs primitive-leafed as denizens
of primeval forests stretched lingual fronds
unheard into my self-absorption; coded discs
were hammered into poles; a bomb-black pod
hung high against the looping wires. Somewhere,
people as strange and licensed by my sloth
nod in the smoke of chambers on my behalf.'

Snow Pieces

Clouds are whirling, clouds are scurrying,
Dark is the sky, and dark the night.
                        Pushkin: *Demons*

1.

That night
as we returned through canyons
of snow

at last
you began to speak, your words
shyly

testing
the perimeters of my
wary

silence.
We carried this new secret
towards

soldiers
imported to keep the roads
open

to food
and influence. Their blank eyes
heard all.

2.

Long stoles of snow
charm the hedges

trembling a conjuror's risk
along the branches.

In some uneasy houses
a room is lit

as though something
cannot be appeased

but must stay awake
as its gift to the night.

3.

The world queues for milk
in a bonhomie of incandescent need.
We join the scratchy newsreels

that flicker with foreign distress.
The milkman magics and bestows
and declares emptiness.

He throws returns into the snow mound
like spears of ice,
like transparent bangers in a white mash.

The copters poise like saviours overhead
and land elsewhere.
We push home through sully and slush,

primitives in an arctic zoo,
to dead phones and the last candle.
We are impressed by this show of power.

The surgery is bizarre: where usually
women perch, hissing at fretful children,
sit men, ranged as if to make
a public admission beneath the mortal
posters of named certainties.
A great wave of snow has lifted them
onto a high remote region of glittering
pointlessness, where they can hear their heart
and all its misses, and what the night dreams
cannot be dispersed through a stiff agenda,
or lunchtime gin, or an office of banter
and chatter. Little discoveries
of need and failure shine in the icy sun
on the blocked roads that once pumped them
to trains and motorways. They hug them here,
wondering what words to find when the moment
of their called name comes. Doctor, I...
Doctor, when...Doctor, I feel...

There are strange zones of existence
on the margins of every system,
exclusions, rejections. They are corralled with fear,
remaindered like unacceptable texts.
Their virtue is to grow savagely unappeased
and to pulse like a lighthouse beyond the rocks of their exile.
On personal maps, they are labelled 'Unfulfilled Dreams',
'Dreadful Mistake', 'Abandoned Ideals',
like a Victorian gallery of anecdotes,
unvisited, discredited. But nagging.

Elsewhere, behind bland offices and shopfronts,
Villon in his cell is wrestling with truth, although tomorrow
his tongue will blacken on the gibbet
and photographs prove that he never was.
The deep-dug hole and dogged mouth are glimpsed
each time we open our study door and enter...

The snowplough performs an act of memory,
uncovering a root of lane from the main road.
No longer a wide sweep of passage
but a meander into itself, an inward drift
between white altitudes. Just before twilight
the men perambulate with their children,
oddly convalescent, tentative-footed,
in this world of wholly Now. Abandoned cars
brood like amnesiacs in their white cells.
It is as if a war has finished and we inherit
the full responsibility of possible futures.
One man stops to shake a bloom of snow
from a hawthorn onto his child, with a grave
attentiveness, as if this is what he knows
now he was born for.

                        I have a vision
in this snowlit silence, of the released
prisoners of the world entering again
the streets of their cities, not with amnesty
or provisional warrants of parole, but with
the proclamation 'We need you. We were mistaken.
Without you we are diminished.' And of
each person as a city where released prisoners,
not with amnesty, or provisional warrants of parole . . .

The men are struggling with the embarrassment
of looking at one another, of acknowledging
'I am here. This is me. I can hear my heart
and all its misses. I am nakedly ashamed
and delighted.' They avert their gaze, study
the children, the snow, the cars. But when
their eyes meet, they blaze, and it is like
embracing . . . .

Father and Son

His reality became the form he achieved, the form
that does not lament transience or the vicissitudes
of history, but transmits an existence in peace.
Peter Handke: *Slow Homecoming*

My Father Begins to Tell his Story

A day arrives whose maples
shadow a room, their sway
distorting moons and waterfalls
that gazed their fictions from a wall

for years into a life. A magisterial chair
still fosters the unrenounced blue stare
that presided marriage, staunched its own
proclivities in children, and froze

itself in fury. But now the cheek
loosens with a wing of doubt. The eyes
curdle with the smoulderings of a tamped
story. What master is dethroned,

what rod snapped, to release this falter
of starved history from the locked dark?
Something approaches like a small conquest
while there is still time, while there remains

a father to confess, a son to hear,
softly merged by the enlacements
of Spring-haunted branches. One man
speaks for all when he revisits his silences.

My Father Reveals a Photograph

i.

A sepia tent
mushrooms from leafwrack:

at once nostalgia
and a covert never quitted

where a boy crouches in vigil
at the taped flap.

He stares through a shaking
loss of focus,

his needs making their arrangements
stone-blind, butting at the light.

His palm extends
towards emptiness.

His mind is the ocean
on which it drifts.

ii.

I stand in the valley of his gaze
where a fleet of headstones

drove at him under the moon
full tilt on their bone sea;

where a hunting owl
vanished like gunsmoke

and an apricot bruise
ripened into a sun.

Faded eyes
watch me that once

admitted the metaphors
of their own richness.

                    iii.

He pitched his tent in the coal-hole
on his return, deep

in the webbed dust, stowing
the remains of trotters and bread

on the high shelf
where he had filched them.

He sallied, armoured and curt,
into the provenance of his dying

father, battening welds of unlikelihood
inside an album and a heart.

My Father's First Job

He bore small walnut casks
fleetly across London

like Hermes, to customers
in high, chrome flats.

He hovered as they
swung lids on bronze hinges,

cupped ears like aviators
and fiddled crystal with fine probes.

When they smiled dreamily
it was all right, a tip,

and dismissal.
At last, his master beckoned him

to the bench, set
world-excluding horn over his ears,

and finger-and-thumbed a magic.
Glimpsed universes

trailed orchestras
and news. He travelled

henceforth like Tantalus,
excluded from a tasted

joy, tormented
by the unheard vastness of his gift.

My Father's Second Job

The gutters pig-pink.
Hands numb with lumped

innards. 4 am light.
Ultimate reduction

where women are dismembered
and no-one cares a fuck.

Iron-shod clogs
drag from ham to ham,

pig's skull to crimped tripes,
rippled brains to liver-slicks.

This mortuary
underpins Sundays,

river picnics, extravagant
leisured visions.

It breeds under nails, exudes
from pores. It guts

language of condition and purpose.
Its gaslight closeted you

in mountainous darkness,
flashed faces

of interred professionals.
Yet, one dawn,

braving the jeers,
she was there,

with film-star's legs
and jaunty pillbox hat:

your wife, my mother, who
led you to whisper

and touch, and the dared
instinct of redress.

My Father Talks of his Life and Death

All my life the presence of unlocatable
enemies; a whisper of malediction;
a ghostly hand guiding my life off-centre.

At my shoulder a timid god to placate;
in my bed a crooked conjuror of dreams
of fall whenever the day soared.

In the benevolence of my masters
a cage with a door swung open.
In their praise, the click of a lock.

My choice a rat's choice in a maze.
My prizes fringed with distant laughter.
My journeys predicted on secret maps.

I have emerged from their hands on this final
upwards slope. They can ignore
this unprofitable zero lunging at the air.

I remember you told me once of Villon,
wrestling for truth the night before the gibbet.
I have emerged into that, the cell whose keepers

no longer bother to observe. It is dark,
without whispers. I begin to walk
a long perspective which is purely mine.

A View from the Boundary:
for Stephen, soon to go abroad

An air of loss is streaming
at appalling speed
around this planet

rapt in this small
unmoving afternoon
Which is like being a father

who has not told his story
or invited yours
Which is more than red toys

raced on the carpet
and whittled miniature bats
for dead cricketers

on fag cards
or staring together
at terns on a windy coast

Which is more than poems
a creaking attic of poems
poised over your childhood

Now I have the boundary
and at my shoulder a profuse blackbird
and a view of lost skills

and a view of skills too late
acquired and the shock
of that swoop of yours

by which you announce yourself
This game accepts you
more than I ever did

I gave attention to nothing
but emblems
I froze the flame

for its meaning
A leaf casually falling
had to be perfected

by my grief
I never asked
Who are you

It was always
Where are you going
And now you are going

Soon you will not turn
when a bowler turns
but continue walking

across the outfield
over the boundary
quite out of sight

and into my mind
where I have always talked best
One November day

I saw on a hazel
white nuts in green
frills and tiny

clenched catkins both
there both
with a way to go

but both there
And I am both son and
father and that is

the flow we must
bite to the core
or taste nothing

which has been my taste
who have missed so many
boats in contemplating

perfect horizons
It is not enough
the opening of

sealed letters
for comfort
in estranged rooms

I have done that
It defines hell
A baffled part

of the whole story
of which this is
my stuttering start

like that bowler's
first steps whose run
will end in triumph

or temporary
redeemable setback
in a context

of adored imperfection
Above us as you play
a star of silver a plane

dwindles to nothing
as we do
silently while not seeming to move

Silently while not seeming to move
I have been approaching you
as my father unseen

for years arrived
one afternoon in my
authoritative green

armchair an old
upright man at last
stooping to admit

words to himself and me
'mistake' and 'dreamed'
and 'wish' and 'waste'

Man hands on misery
to man when he does
not hand himself

which means
I trust you
which means love

if anything does
And this is not to shoulder
and stagger with

another's confession
bidden to run
for him burdened

with his paraphernalia
when he could not
run himself

It is preparing
for complete death
leaving no ghost-

breeding scraps
no haunted
corridors in

the breathing house
It is to free
the steps of the living

from wading waters
of regret
We must re-invent

rituals for our
great concerns
starting with

holding one another
before journeys
taken alone

and learning to say
goodbye with proper
quittance

and if our only
myth is a quiet
game eccentrically

played where quirks
and lapses and luck
subsume themselves

to a small harmony
in a brief time
between an empty

field and an
empty field it is
no less a proper place

for needs to brood
upon themselves
and for a father

to begin to ask
forgiveness and say
Fare well

Shadowings

Et le Splendide-Hôtel fut bâti dans le chaos de glaces
et de nuit du pôle.

Rimbaud: *Illuminations*

1.

The backbone of the team. A stocky, pugnacious winghalf.
To labour, to sweat, to relieve, to serve.

Far away on the green strips waited the wingers, poised,
unsullied. When they received, they swerved and dallied
in self-regarding artistry, pursuing deeply personal
goals.

Already one of them was eyed with suspicion by the German
teacher lumbered with team management and an increment
that was a hostage to success.

2.

My headaches were very eloquent and sometimes a year long.
But their language was too cryptic. Authorities scanned
the irrelevant dictionaries of sinus and brain-waves. My
belly, too, had much to say, but it chose its moments.

Once, at Christmas, Dr Lesnovitch bent over my armchair.
Behind him stood the interrupted table of red beet and
stilton and mausoleum cake. His eyes looked into mine
with the beginnings of understanding as he pronounced
'nervous dyspepsia'.

He advised against the beetroot if pickled.

3.

Where we were clothed in our customary jackets of solemn
black, scrolled silver with a circumspect motto from the
Age of Bronze, that other came in flaring red.

We turned to meet him, gleeful with the secrets of initiation.
His blond head needed to be twisted down into the drinking
basin and bruised with water.

'Is that all?'

He brushed the drops from his jacket where they trembled
like mercury and told me of subtle and prolonged ceremonies
elsewhere.

4.

One morning, a black man paused at the end of the street.

When he did not return, it was said that, after all, this
was the kind of thing that could be expected now. Nonetheless,
it would be just as well to know if there was a Council
policy.

Other arrivals became the focus of attention: a maroon Wyvern
with small silver flutes; an old Mayflower with the gleam
of lead, its boxy edges still keen. These were a taunt,
parked at the kerb, or setting out conspicuously on
Sundays, leaving their spaces behind them.

5.

As the stroked greenfly exudes sweetness; as autumn
delivers the fruit-tree of its fruit; so at the end
of every term they opened their hands and a report
dropped plumb.

Without blemish, except for a large number of absences
due to headache and 'nervous dyspepsia', this was added
to the rest that had been laid down like apples against
a winter. Occasionally, a hushed relative was granted
a view.

Like tribute-money, these earned me the freedom to be
miserable without interference.

6.

The man who owned the Wyvern also owned one medal. Not a
campaign star, not a hat badge, but a proof of singular
courage, sunk in green baize inside a blue leather box.
On mornings after he had come back drunk, or after he had
provoked a fight about fences or noise or nothing, his wife
displayed this medal, passing it round to be handled.

One day, all three disappeared: car, medal and man. The
women rallied to her defeat. The men gathered under the
silver gaslamps, opening their hands towards the darkness
in gestures ambiguous with dismissal and blessing.

Chess 1950

Pawn to King Four. All I knew.
Then Pawn to Queen Three.
Hunched opposite,
you taught me nothing

and beat me solid
game after game. Night after night.
Endless Slim Whitman
wailing a lost love,

endless finger-rolls
sweetening the air.
Poor sod, said my mother,
he doesn't know where she is.

Gambits, sacrifices,
your trembling hands
played them all.
Against me they won.

Opposite you
a new school tie
playing by the book.
The first page of the book.

Q.E.D.

When Taffy exhorted us
to give up bus-seats to women
'because there are often things happening to them
which we can't understand'

we looked at each other in wild surmise!
The more so as his eyes
swam in watery vagueness
and his chalk-stiff fingers throbbed the desk.

We wandered around quite stunned.
We thought of the high dark shelves in airing-cupboards
where mothers reached.
We hung at bus-stops and scanned the girls for clues.

He never told us more.
He resumed his fearful passion for thin lines
and equal-signs ranged one below the other.
Never again that throat-bunched tenderness,

that vision of unspeakable suffering
and the lyricism of male duty.
But the angles and curves of his geometry
were forever a muttered code at which we trembled.

History 'O' Level

The French are all very well
when on the attack, but when their backs
are to the wall, they collapse.
Hence Alsace-Lorraine.

Disraeli was a Jew. His name
declares it. He was flashy
and suspect. Gladstone never did
those things with whores. He tried to save them.

There were no necrophiliac Pre-Raphaelites.
No pre-pube knocking-shops. The Boer War
was fought on unbelievably difficult
terrain. Rhodes (who was also a left arm

Yorkshireman who went in first and last
for England) was no spiv or thug
but an educator, a bearer of the torch
handed on to us by the Romans.

Those pink places are not scars
but where law is, and democracy.
And the copperplate that blazons this
grew from a Yorkshire Grammar School

where life was real, not like here
in the pulpy south. Next year think hard
before choosing against the discipline
of History, where you learn to discriminate.

Headmaster

'More Shelleyan gestures, Jones?'
Then a morning across the bells and breaks
wrestling with my wish to resign
a prefect's tasselled cap.

I was the angel of light,
he black with experience and compromise.
He sent me out once to buy a packet of Olivier.
I couldn't bring myself to offer one of mine.

On my side were Joyce, James Dean,
and a vague rive gauche:
white-faced black-haired women
and irrefutable epigrams.

He stood no chance.
At mid-day he admitted telephone calls,
rose, shook my hand, and said
'For my sake make one lyric that lasts.'

What did not last was his memory of me.
Twenty years later, that bristling
energy clamped into hieratic
chairbound splendour by a wrecked heart,

he gazed at me as into an empty sky.
Even my name was vapour vanishing.
He had too much future on his mind.
I saw then how he was forever

one of those faces at my shoulder
wincing or smiling at every word,
one of those I had to please or placate.
The ground control of every flight.

My River

All childhoods deserve a river
loitering through. Mine was brown Brent.
A field away and worlds away,
bending round and brushing flakey banks,

little spins upon itself like a brooding
man chuckling, and the green sleeked
hair of beautiful drowned girls.
Bald eyes of golfballs stared

from its unreachable shallows.
On Christmas Day it was an insouciant
cool stroller through the hothouse
bloat of groans and burnt tangerine-peel.

It understood my first love,
accompanying me like a Tchaikovsky clarinet.
Embedded in its deep grass
it taught me staring and the length of afternoons.

It churned or shivered like my spine
and was the slow feel of holidays.
It dreamed India for me with its kingfishers.
The secret untouchable soul grew under its willows.

Sleeplessness recalling it became a slow glide
towards invisible distances.
O it was all wellbeing, and stopped at an orchard
that sired small apples behind unbroachable wire.

Near Greenford 1951

Like a vision it was unaccountable.
I parted branches and there it was,
totally absorbed with itself.
In old cream, with a fringed baldness,

the bowler six times looped a slow ball
like a deeply considered question,
and six times the batsman in his plum cap
leaned very attentively and returned an answer.

Six times. And time did not matter,
was utterly elsewhere.
There were fielders listening
and distant waiting batsmen in shadow

under trees listening. It was like staring
into deep water
at unexplained subtleties of light.
I was achingly excluded in another element.

Though I found my way back
it was never back to that:
perfect exposition, perfect refutation,
and something beyond them both, winning.

The Offer, The Refusal

An inordinate Rolls de-created our street
to its cardboard and tarred lumps. It stopped
with a hint of shudder. This was the Boss.
He extruded a starched smile aimed at no-one.

Exiled to the kitchen, we craned at the hidden voices.
When he left, it was with embarrassed delicacy
as though someone should have tipped someone.
The car's velvet wake stirred a river of faces.

For the first and last time, my father gathered us
round. He said he'd been offered 'because I'm valued'
a loan to buy a real brick house. And had refused it.
We spent days stunned with grief and admiration.

Meanwhile, my father forked the passive earth
with vicious lacerating twists, brooding on how,
night after night, year after year, he had dreamed
his dismissal, after a prolonged trial for treachery.

After Tempest

Il faut imaginer Sisyphe heureux.
Camus: *Le Mythe de Sisyphe*

Four Poems of Noëlle

1.

You found me among rubble
with the trace of a finger.
You separated
my enemies from my body
and shredded them with invective.

You tossed the Empire, all its
monuments and stratagems,
pomp and rigor, high in the air;
all my bitter envisaged redress,
my cold meal of revenge,

like a bomb of love. Furious against
the yearning creature's collusion
with its unnatural enemies,
the alignment with self-pity,
the pact with a wheedling past,

you doused the false lights
and scattered my fence of words.
'Don't curl like dead peel
over bitterness. Don't dance
to dead strings. Let's uncage eternity!'

2.

Born by the mythic sea
that witnesses and forgets
everything, except
what lingers in the air
when all the towers have fallen,

you are the inconsequent child
who compromises nothing, dancing
along the line of masks. You swat
the world's news like a cloud of gnats
and will listen only to the heart.

When I went missing, holing out
in ramshackle plywood under a neglected
orchard, that was where you were,
waiting to find me. 'Where else,' you smiled,
'Where else on earth was it possible to be?'

3.

A Moment from Algeria

I conjure, here
by this whistling woodfire,
your schoolgirl's insouciant
pirouette into the Square

as volleys unbuckled
a soldier from his trappings
and his shocked eyes
caught as he fell

the echo of a lifetime's
yearning cry: you, in white
sprigged with lilac and rose,
flowering in a city

where ideal tortured ideal.
And you, what do you recall?
– 'His eyes' bequest, the unaligned
unanswerable desire of creatures.'

4.

Tonight, there is a different noise:
speculative, like knuckles enquiring at a door
as if fearful it might be opened.
You are typing. You are gathering yourself

in those small trugs which are poems.
You are walking away down miraculous alleys
through that orchard where the fruit still hangs
to be picked and brought shining back.

You are making those marks like birdprints in snow,
like those faint lines on the grass of the camp
where people stayed, looked into our eyes,
and vanished like Troy. The noise quickens,

steps breaking into a run. I hear you leaving me
for encounters under trees, in a Church,
on a hot, distant shore. You are keeping
rendez-vous after all these years

with the waiting ghosts. Whatever you find,
embrace. They are what I mean
whenever I embrace you. I will be waiting, too,
to be found afresh, enlightened by your journey.

Walk by Storm-Wrecked Wood

White
as chicken-flesh
the scars.

The roots
broached
in walls of flint.

This the day
that chooses
to return

to me
the birds
of memory

from my lost
woodlands –
how they

sang
and in what
atmospheres.

Autumn

Last week
the house sang
with tempest,
and oaks

fell.
We studied
wreckage,
hearts broken.

Today
in windless
sunlight
leaves patter

and kiss
our hair
with manageable
deaths.

Nature

The thing itself
is silent.
Impatience battens

on the fern,
the mountain,
the tree.

And when
snow falls
it is

not enough.
And yellow
lilies

in a blue
vase
must bear

so much
of a particular
house,

and sunlight
touching them
is burdened.

At Stansted

The barn-roof
settles
in my gaze,

becomes
a curve
of my mind.

And I brought
here
so much,

so much
else
which now

is inches
of curve
of roof.

Snowstorm Viewed from Love

All shapes disband themselves
in this soft explosion:
the unfixed possibilities of the world
whirl and spin their primal courtesies

against the wall-eye of the universe,
deftly alone, untouching:
pure minimals of trees and homesteads;
clear notes of the resounding silence

at the heart of concertos, hectorings,
and consolations. Behind me
you sleep, whiteness
defining your shoulder,

your head received in whiteness,
and, beyond, the empty
whiteness smoothly awaiting
whatever colours I dream.

Tomorrow, I will invite you
to step into the aftermath
of turmoil, where sunlight
fires crystals across a huge

blank, into which our hands
will reach, to build
something like a man or woman
unflinching under a jaunty hat.

I Think of Sisyphus

endlessly resuming his endless task, thrusting
a rock upward on fate's down escalator,
as if, despite all the evidence, there smiles
Sense at the heart of things, that will one day plant

the rock on the summit, leaving only the question
To what end? Each inch – each grudged fraction
of inch – is achievement. Which is the only end.
And Sisyphus is blest, never condemned to stand

in his completed dream, the world applauding
or indifferent, cleaned of his investment
of sweat, the burden of a Nothing on a height
overlooking Nothing. He never knows failure –

the rock is always balanced against the future.
Sisyphus thinks he is asserting Hope. But he
is combatant with Despair. The despair of
gravity, and commonsense, and the laws of proportion.

He yearns as he shoves. On the desirable heights
the gods of limit preside. They cannot kill
Sisyphus, despite the tombstones of their vision.
His visionary eyes stare at his feet. He is